Zoom In on

Native American Leaders

Sequoyah

Jennifer Strand

abdopublishing.com

Published by Abdo Zoom™, PO Box 398166, Minneapolis, Minnesota 55439.

Printed in the United States of America, North Mankato, Minnesota
052017
092017

THIS BOOK CONTAINS RECYCLED MATERIALS

Cover Photo: Burstein Collection/Corbis Historical/Getty Images
Interior Photos: Burstein Collection/Corbis Historical/Getty Images, 1, 18; iStockphoto, 4, 6–7, 10–11; Sue Ogrocki/AP Images, 5; Gerry Embleton/North Wind Picture Archive, 7; Everett Historical/Shutterstock Images, 8–9; Library of Congress, 10, 19; North Wind Picture Archive, 12; Shutterstock Images, 13; British Cartoon Prints Collection/Library of Congress, 14; Morphart Creation/Shutterstock Images, 15; Carol M. Highsmith/Carol M. Highsmith Archive/Library of Congress, 16

Editor: Emily Temple
Series Designer: Madeline Berger
Art Direction: Dorothy Toth

Publisher's Cataloging-in-Publication Data
Names: Strand, Jennifer, author.
Title: Sequoyah / by Jennifer Strand.
Description: Minneapolis, MN : Abdo Zoom, 2018. | Series: Native American leaders | Includes bibliographical references and index.
Identifiers: LCCN 2017931234 | ISBN 9781532120268 (lib. bdg.) | ISBN 9781614797371 (ebook) | 9781614797937 (Read-to-me ebook)
Subjects: LCSH: Sequoyah, 1770?-1843--Juvenile literature. | Cherokee Indians--Biography--Juvenile literature. | Cherokee language--Writing--Juvenile literature. | Cherokee language--Alphabet--Juvenile literature.
Classification: DDC 975.004/975570/092 [B]--dc23
LC record available at http://lccn.loc.gov/2017931234

Table of Contents

Introduction

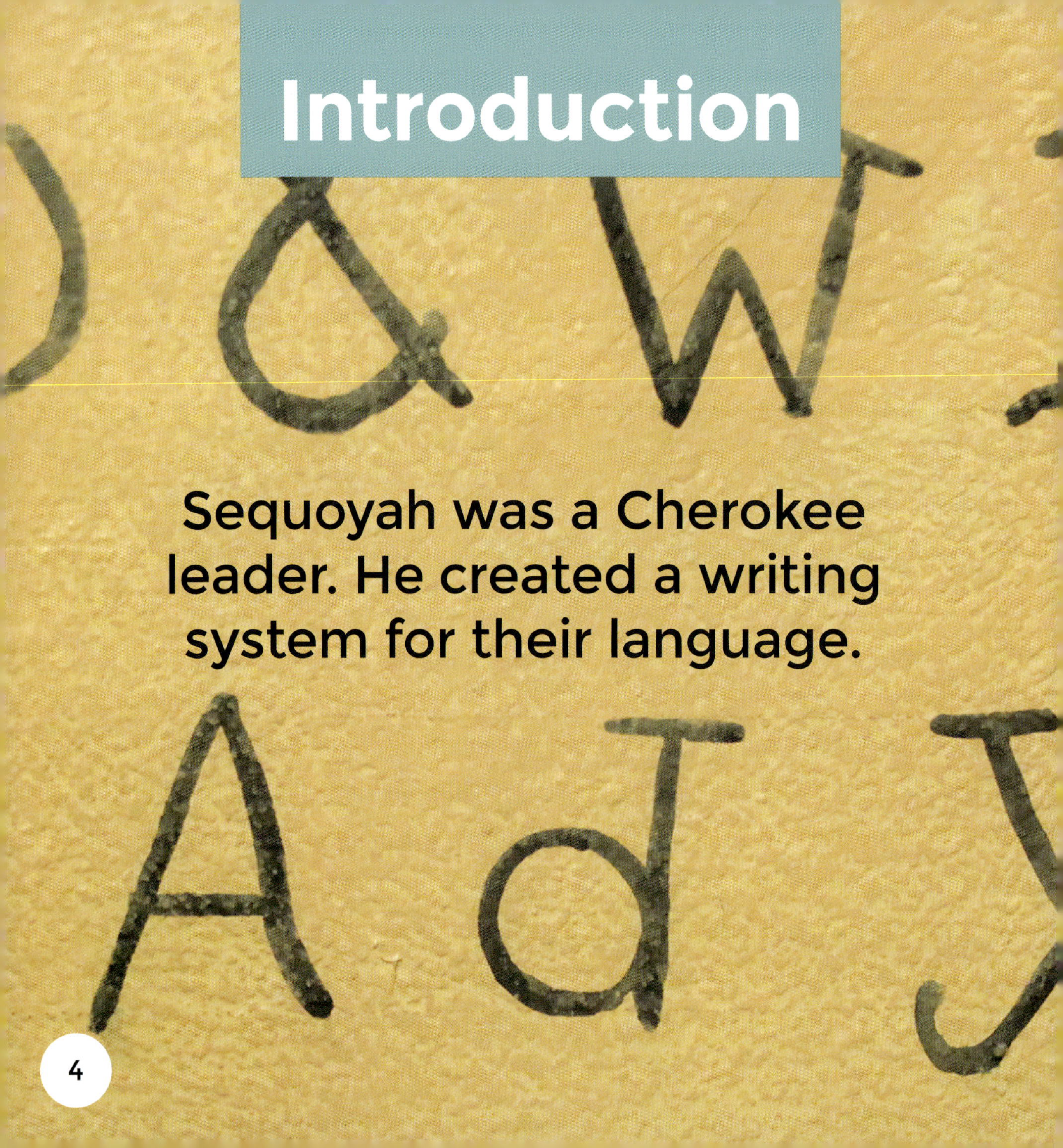

Sequoyah was a Cherokee leader. He created a writing system for their language.

His work helped the Cherokee people learn and share ideas.

Early Life

Sequoyah was likely born in the early 1760s. His father was a fur **trader**.

His mother was part of the Cherokee **tribe**.

Leader

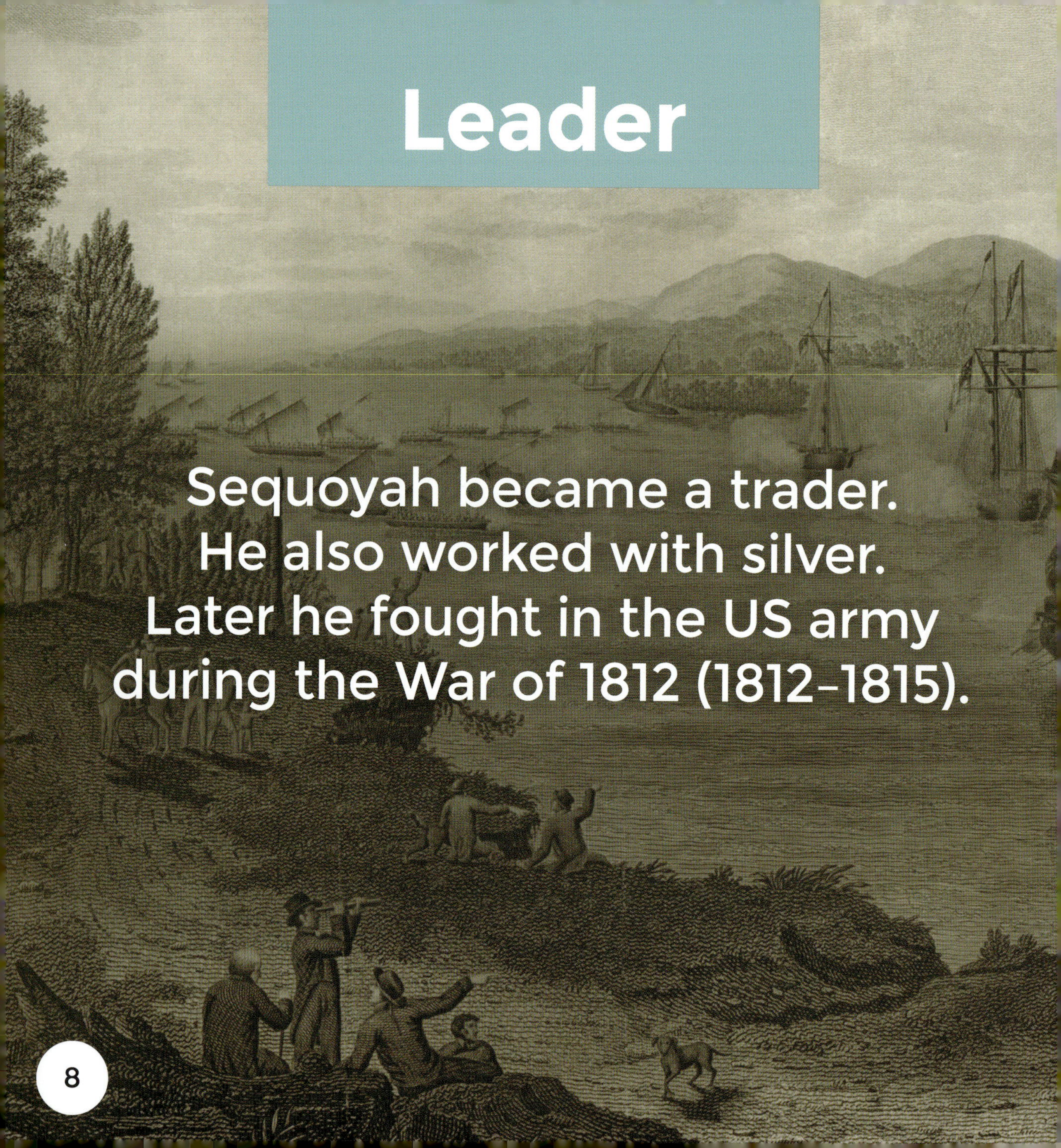

Sequoyah became a trader. He also worked with silver. Later he fought in the US army during the War of 1812 (1812–1815).

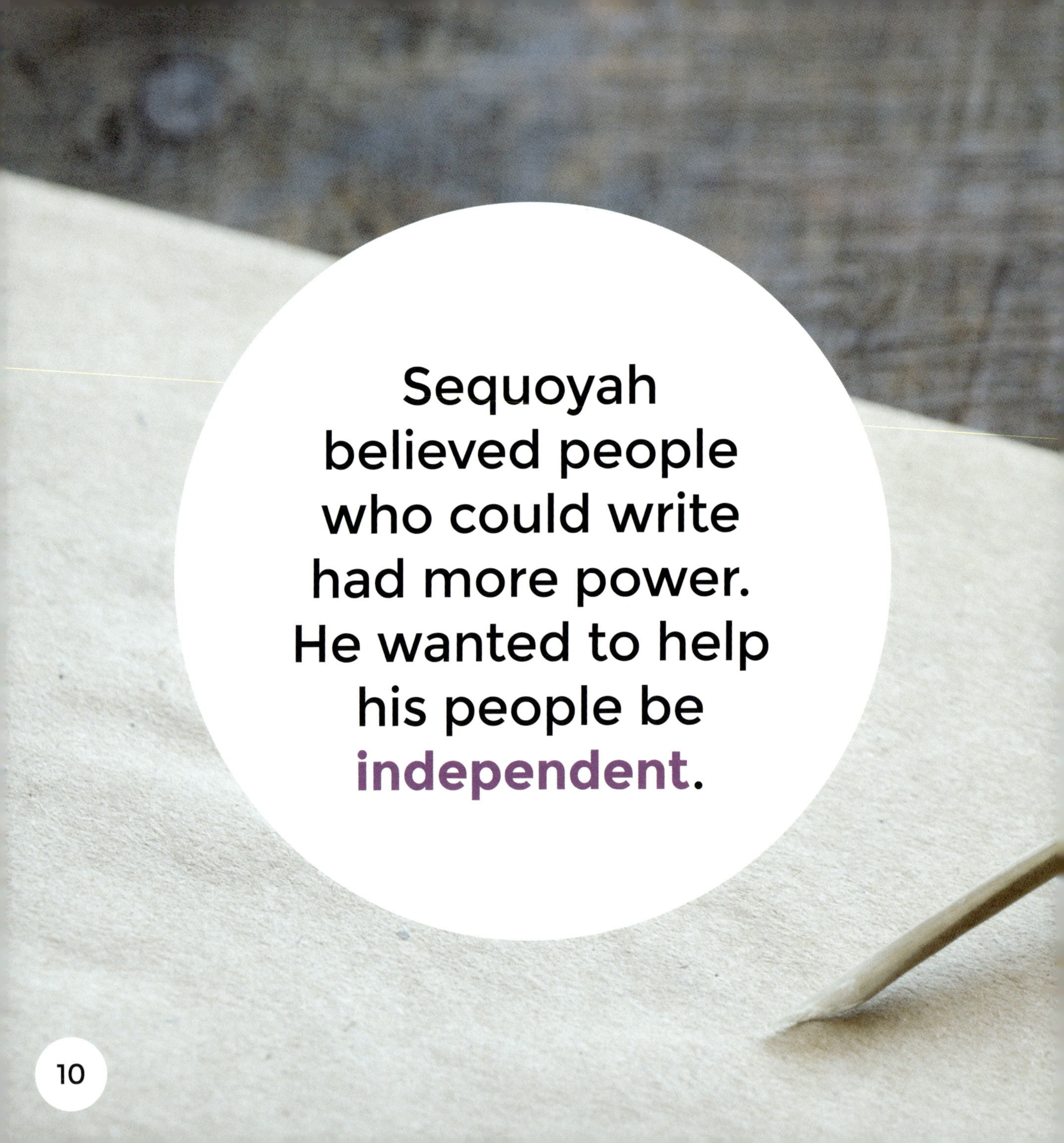

Sequoyah believed people who could write had more power. He wanted to help his people be **independent**.

So he made a system of writing for their language.

History Maker

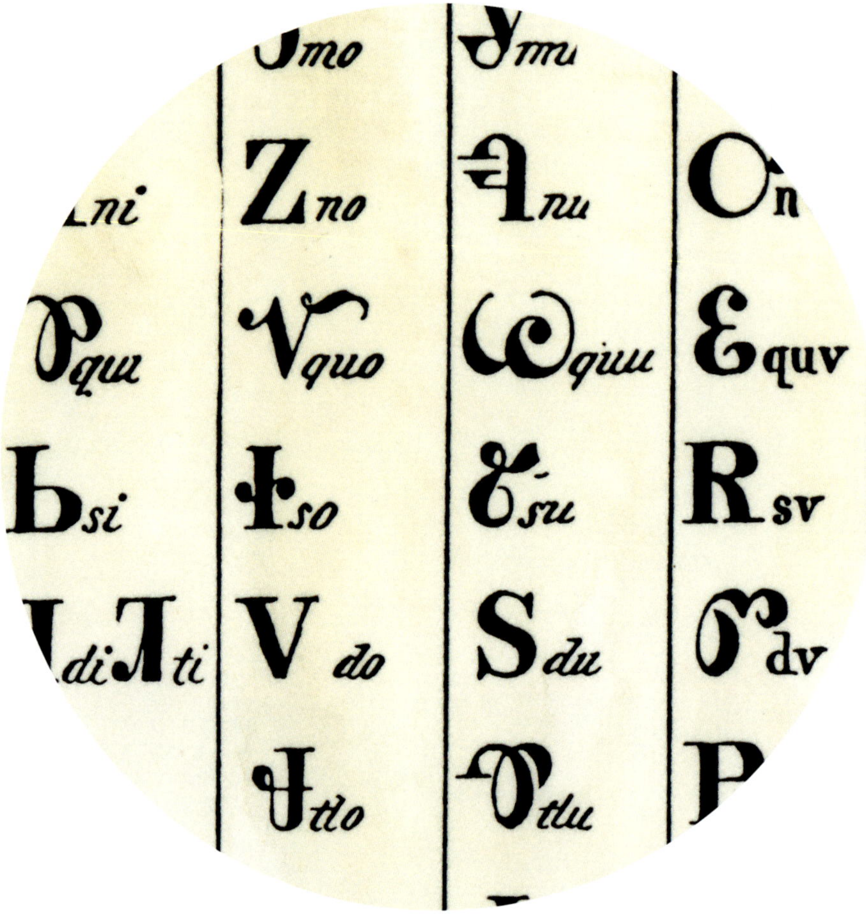

Sequoyah made an alphabet.
It used 86 **symbols**.

Each symbol stood for a **syllable**.

In 1821, he showed the alphabet to Cherokee leaders.

He sent a message to his daughter. She read it. This showed his work was a success.

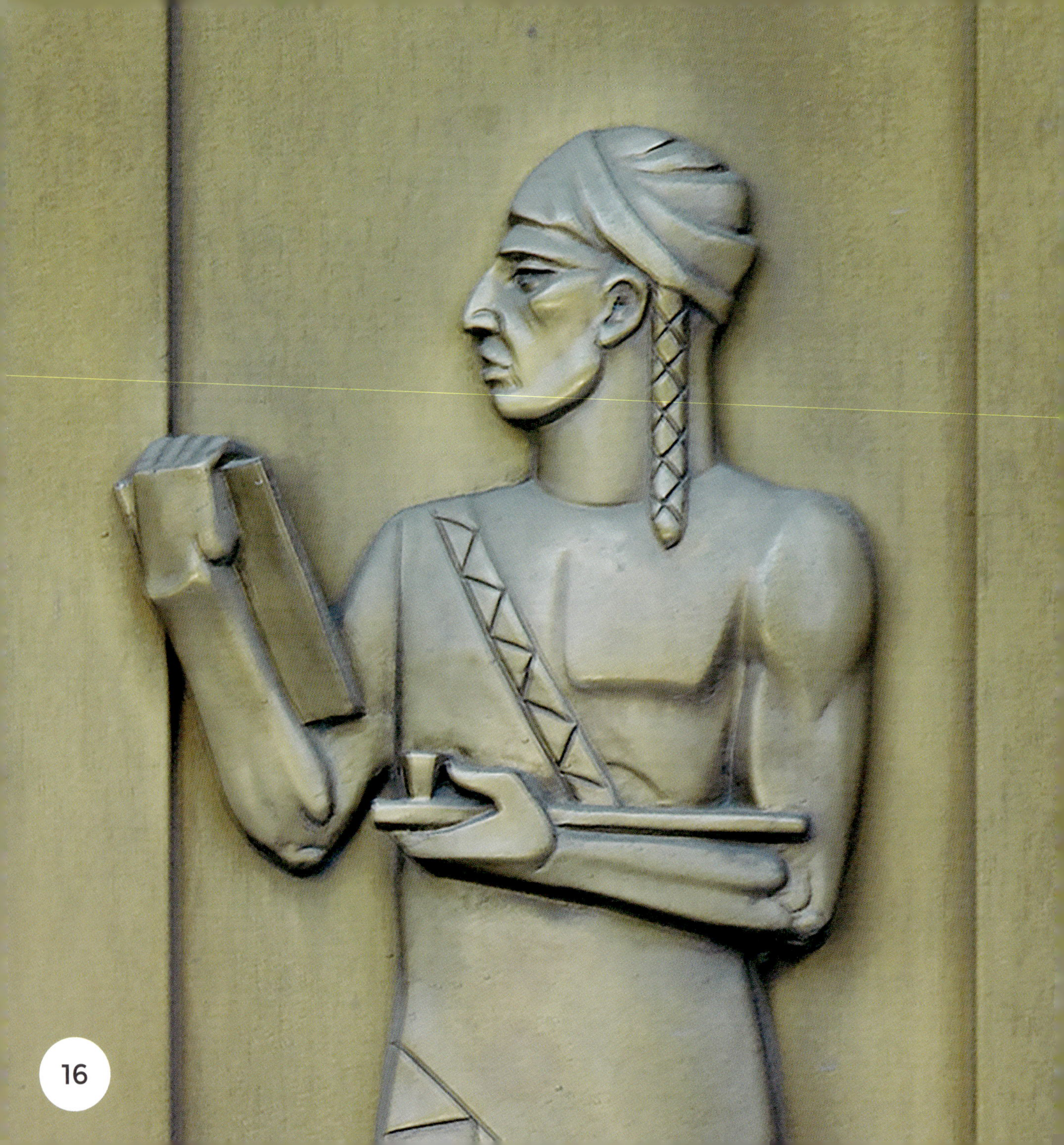

Sequoyah taught others to use the alphabet. Many Cherokees learned the alphabet. They used it to read and write.

Legacy

Sequoyah died in 1843. His writing system was easy to use.

PROTECTION

CHEROKEE PHŒNIX.

VOL. I. NEW ECHOTA, THURSDAY APRIL 10, 1828.

Many Cherokees taught his writing system in their schools. They used it in books and newspapers, too.

Quick Stats

Sequoyah

Born: around the 1760s, the exact date is not known

Birthplace: Taskigi, which is now Tuskegee, Tennessee

Wife: Sally Waters

Known For: Sequoyah invented a way of writing down the Cherokee language.

Died: August 1843

Key Dates

1760s: Sequoyah is born around this time. The exact date is not known.

1809: Sequoyah begins creating his alphabet.

1821: Sequoyah shows his alphabet to the Cherokee council.

1824: The Cherokee Nation gives Sequoyah an important honor.

1828: The *Cherokee Phoenix* is published. It is the first national newspaper in two languages.

1843: Sequoyah dies in August.

Glossary

independent - not ruled or controlled by another person or country.

syllable - one of the sounds that makes up a word.

symbol - an image or object that stands for or means something else.

trader - a person whose job is to buy and sell goods.

tribe - a group of people who share the same culture and beliefs.

Booklinks

For more information on Sequoyah, please visit abdobooklinks.com

Zoom In on Biographies!

Learn even more with the Abdo Zoom Biographies database. Check out abdozoom.com for more information.

Index